A Children's Guide to Spring Wildflowers

by Rebecca A. Doty

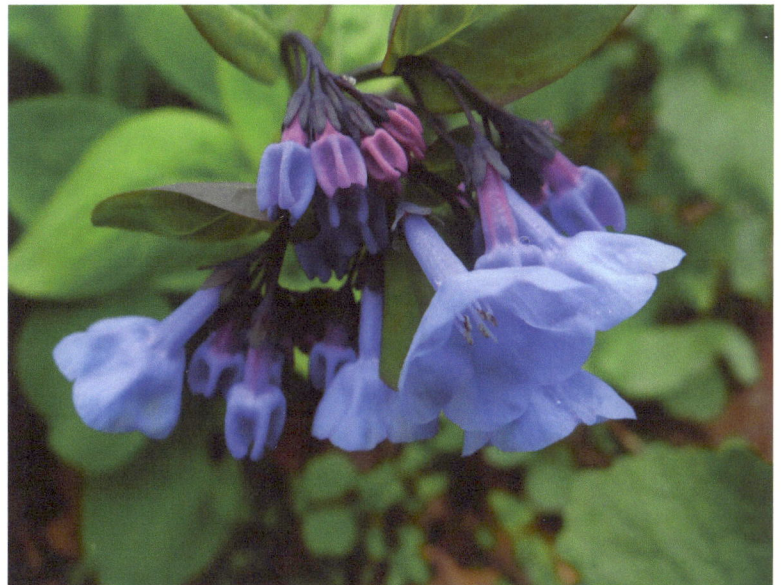

Quillwort Publishing

To my favorite flowers, Linnaea and Lily

A Children's Guide to Spring Wildflowers written by Rebecca A. Doty
Photographs by Rebecca A. Doty
Published by Quillwort Publishing

ISBN-13: 978-0-692-62065-6
ISBN-10: 0-692-62065-6

Table of Contents

pistil

stamen

petal

sepal

Next time you see a flower, try to find these plant parts.

flower bud

flower

leaf

stem

An Introduction to Spring Wildflowers

Spring wildflowers come up after the winter snow melts. They blanket forest floors for a short time and then disappear until the next year. Why are they only out in the spring? These plants need sunlight to make food. During the summer the leaves of tall trees block much of the sunlight from reaching the forest floor. The leaves of spring wildflowers receive more sunlight during the spring before tree leaves grow back.

This guide will help you identify some common spring wildflowers during your next hike in the woods.

Liverleaf

Liverleaf, or Hepatica, is one of the earliest spring wildflowers. The flowers can be white, lavender, pink, or a lovely blue. They come out of the ground before the leaves. The leaves have a smooth surface, but their **stems** are very hairy. These hairs act like a winter coat. They help keep the plant warm during early spring days.

3

Bloodroot

What a funny name for such a pretty white flower! This plant has one big green leaf that grows around a white flower. It is named bloodroot because when the stems and roots are cut, a bright red-orange liquid comes out. Native Americans may have used these plants to create dye to color clothing and baskets.

4

Skunk Cabbage

Skunk cabbage flowers often come up when there is still snow on the ground. Unlike most plants, skunk cabbage can raise the temperature of their flowers. This can melt the snow around them. Be prepared when you smell a skunk cabbage flower! They smell like rotten meat! The bad smell and warm temperatures attract flies and beetles that **pollinate** the flowers. The leaves of this plant also smell bad when you tear them.

Rue Anemone

Rue anemone is a common wildflower that comes up in early spring. It has smooth leaves and smooth, thin stems. The flowers have between 5 to 10 white or light pink **petals**. Windflower is another name for this plant. On a windy day you can watch as the flowers dance in the wind.

Dutchman's Breeches

What do you think these flowers look like? Do you think they look like upside down pants hanging on a clothesline? They are called Dutchman's breeches. Breeches are a type of stretchy pants. The flowers are mostly white, with a bit of yellow where they open. They are pollinated by bumblebees. Bumblebees have long tongues that reach the **nectar** at the far ends of each flower. Some other insects steal the nectar from these plants. They do this by chewing a small hole where the nectar is, and slurp it up! These insects are called **nectar robbers**.

Squirrel Corn

The flowers of squirrel corn look like little white hearts. The seeds of these plants are interesting. Attached to each seed is a packet of food that ants love to eat. The ants carry the seeds back home, eat the food, and then throw the seeds away in an underground trash pile. This is perfect for the seeds! The seeds are hidden from animals that may eat them. The seeds can grow and produce new flowers. Plants whose seeds are **dispersed** by ants are often found growing together in large clumps.

Trout Lily

Trout lilies grow bright yellow flowers. Attached to a flower are two green leaves that have many brown markings all over them. The leaves are the same color as a type of fish called a brook trout—if you use your imagination! Young trout lily plants only have one leaf. Older trout lily plants will have two leaves and these older plants will flower. There are also white trout lily flowers.

Mayapple

You will notice the leaves of mayapples before you see a flower. The leaves may remind you of little umbrellas. Just imagine a little mouse using these leaves to take shelter from the rain. Most often you will see many shiny mayapple leaves growing in a large circle on the forest floor. These plants are probably all connected by long underground stems. To find a mayapple flower, look for a plant that has two leaves. Where the leaves separate, a flower will develop in early May. Latter in the summer the flower will turn into a green fruit that will ripen. Most parts of mayapple plants are toxic, and eating them can make you very sick!

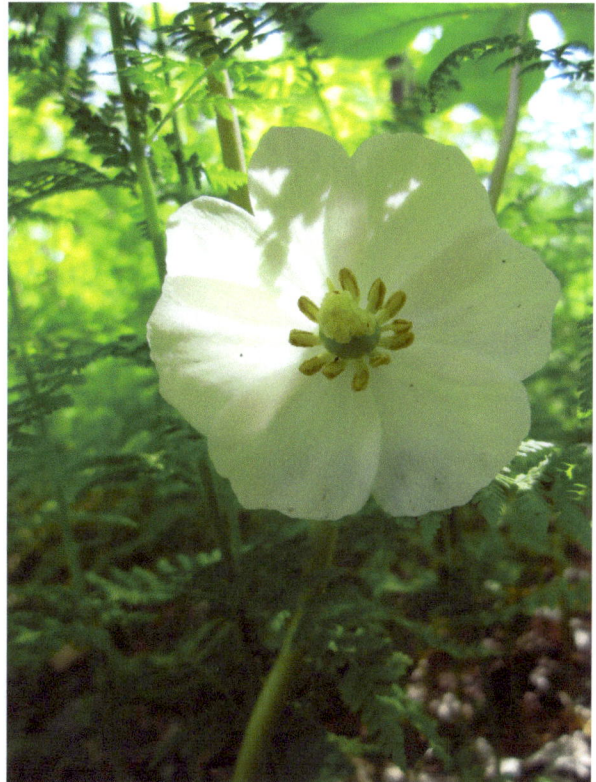

Spring Beauty

Aren't these flowers beautiful? They are called spring beauties. Each flower has five pale pink or white petals that have bright pink lines. The pink lines are **nectar guides**. Nectar guides are patterns on petals that guide pollinators to the nectar and **pollen** a plant makes. You may think of them as being a "runway" for insects to find nectar.

11

Trillium

There are many different types of trillium. Their flowers can be red, purple, white, yellow, or green. Trillium plants are easy to identify. They have three large petals and three green **sepals** that come off of three green leaves. The letters "tri" mean three. Red trilliums usually have maroon flowers that smell bad. Like skunk cabbage, they are pollinated by flies. Great white trilliums have large white flowers that do not smell, and are pollinated by bumblebees. Painted trilliums have white petals that have pink markings on the bases.

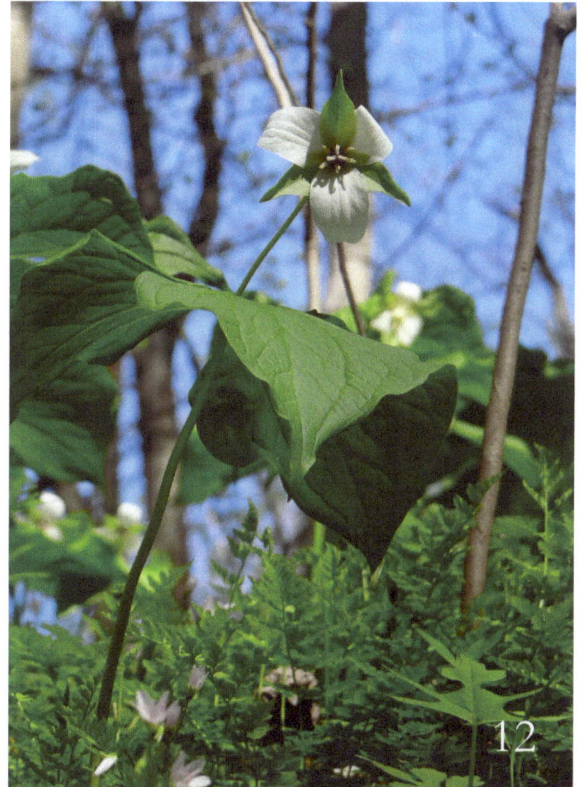

a rare red trillium with white petals

12

Cut-leaved Toothwort

Many plants have the letters "wort" in their names. It is an old word that means plant. Cut-leaved toothwort is also named after its jagged or toothed leaves. To identify this plant look at the leaves and flowers. Each flower has four petals that are white or sometimes light pink. Bees and butterflies like to visit this plant to get nectar.

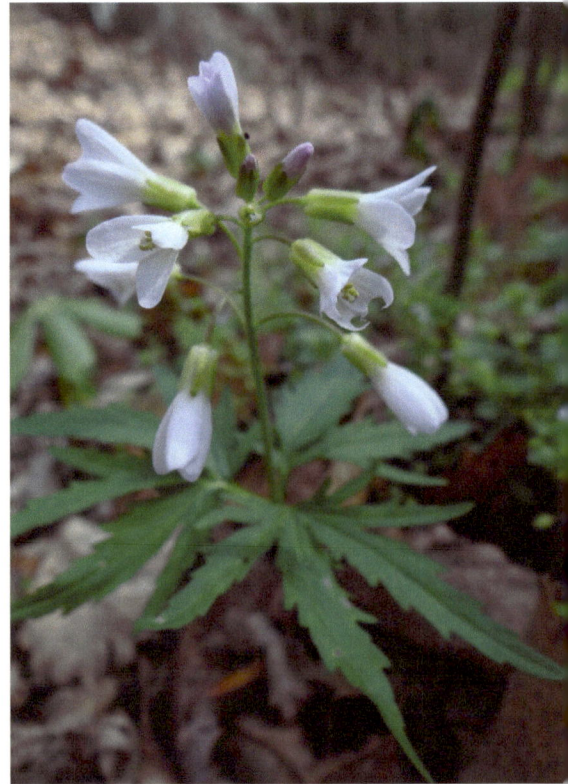

13

Blue Cohosh

When blue cohosh first comes out of the ground it has a purple stem with folded up leaves. The leaves will expand and support a series of tiny flowers. Some of these flowers are maroon in color, but others look yellow or pale green. The small size and subdued colors of these special flowers make them easy to miss. Native Americans and early settlers used blue cohosh for medicine. However, you should never eat this plant. Kids have gotten sick from eating the blue berries this plant grows.

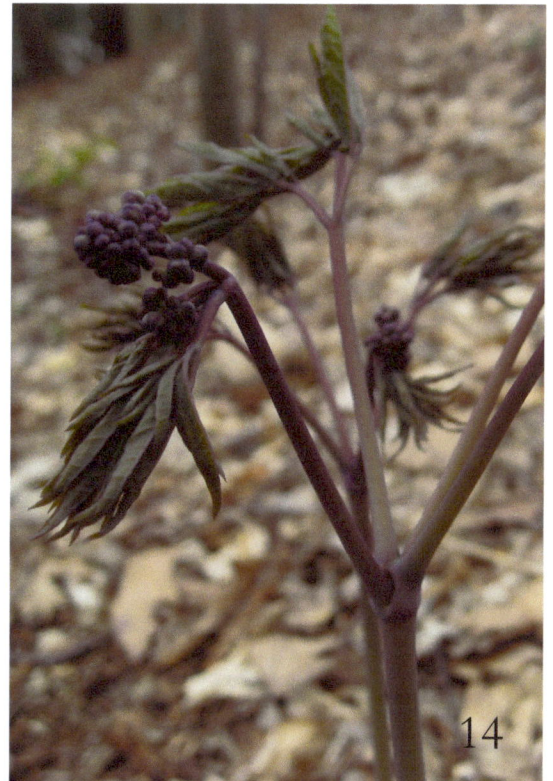

14

Wild Geranium

If you visit a garden store you may find red and pink geraniums for sale. People often plant these flowers in their gardens, but they are different from the ones in a forest. Wild geraniums naturally grow in forests. They have five pink or purple petals that attract bees, flies, and beetles. Notice that the leaves and stems of wild geraniums are covered with many small hairs, just like the geraniums you find in garden stores. These small hairs stop animals from eating the plant.

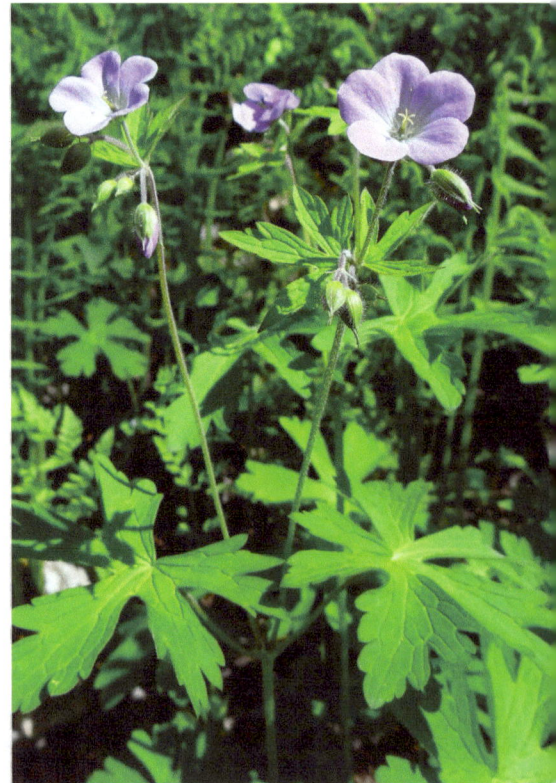

Virginia Bluebells

These pretty blue flowers are called Virginia bluebells. Do they look like little bells to you? The **flower buds** start off pink, turn purple, and finally blue. Many people like these flowers so much they plant them in gardens. If you want bluebells in your garden, please buy them from a garden store. You should never take plants from the woods back to your home. If everyone took plants home, there wouldn't be any left to enjoy in the woods!

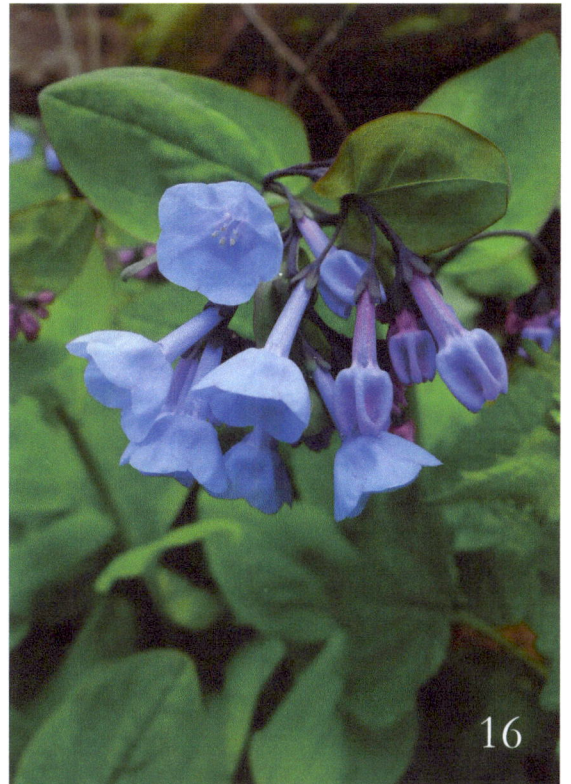

Wild Blue Phlox

If you see a patch of wild blue phlox, stop and smell the flowers! They have a nice smell that butterflies, moths, and bees like. Although they are called wild blue phlox, they may be blue, purple, or even pink. Each flower has five petals that form a tube at the base. If you gently touch a stem of this plant you may find it to be sticky and hairy. Some animals may avoid eating this plant because of the sticky stems.

17

Jack-in-the-Pulpit

What an interesting looking flower! Actually, this isn't one flower, but a collection of many tiny flowers surrounded by a strange looking leaf. This plant is called Jack-in-the-pulpit, but many of these flowers are girl flowers. The boy flowers make lots of pollen. If a **pollinator** carries pollen from a boy flower to a girl flower, the girl flower may produce bright red berries in the summer.

18

Wild Ginger

Look at this unusual flower. Isn't it hairy? You will find this maroon flower hiding along the forest floor under two heart shaped leaves. Even though we call this plant wild ginger, please don't eat it! It can make you sick. This is a different ginger from the one people buy at the food store.

Violets

You do not need to go into the woods to find violets. Some violets grow in people's yards. They have heart shaped leaves and their flowers have five petals. Two of the petals point up on top of the flower, two petals point sideways, and one petal points down to the ground. Not all violets are violet in color. There are also yellow, blue, and white violets.

Wild Columbine

Wild columbine has flowers that are red on the outside, but yellow on the inside. Do you see the five long tubes at the end of the flower? This plant makes nectar at the ends of these tubes. Hummingbirds like to visit red flowers with long tubes. So if you find wild columbine in the woods, keep an eye out for hummingbirds!

21

Squawroot

In the spring squawroot stems come out of the ground and grow many small cream colored flowers. You won't find any green leaves with these flowers. Without green leaves this plant is not able to make food. Instead, this plant steals food from nearby oak tree roots. Squawroot is a plant parasite! It needs oak trees in order to survive. If all the oak trees in a forest disappear squawroot will disappear too.

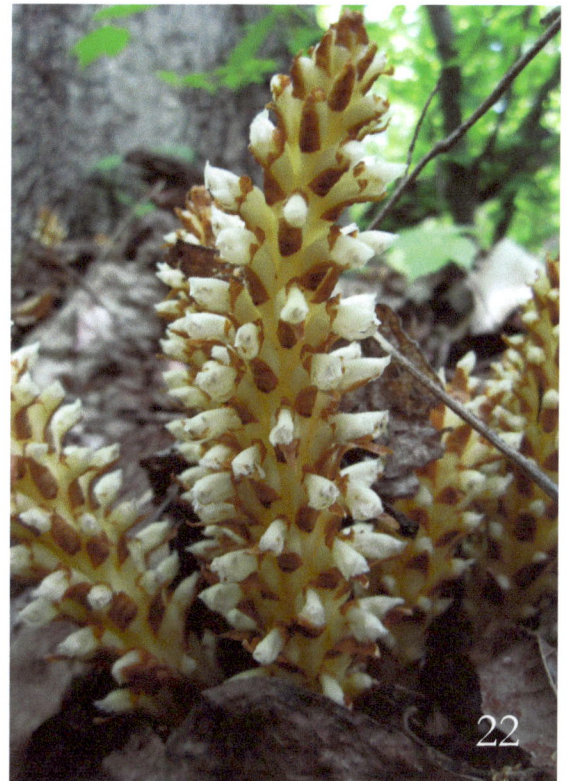

Garlic Mustard

If you crush a leaf of this plant you will smell garlic. This plant is called garlic mustard. Garlic mustard flowers have four white petals. Although these flowers look pretty, this plant is an **invasive plant**. An invasive plant is a plant that takes over a new place and harms the environment. Garlic mustard came from Europe. It grows fast and can hurt many of the native wildflowers you just learned about.

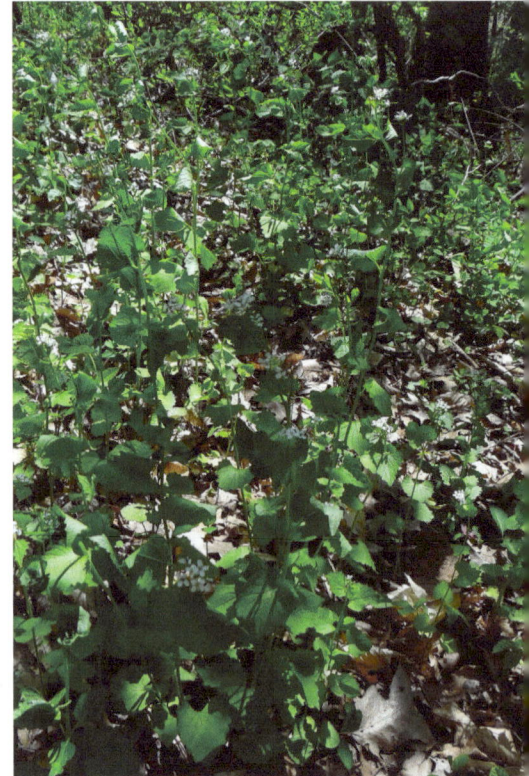

23

Fiddleheads

This is not a flower, but it is another sign that spring is here. This is a young fern, and it will never flower. When young ferns come out of the ground they are curled up. This is why they are called fiddleheads—they look like the very top of a musical instrument called a fiddle.

Flowering Trees

Wildflowers growing on the forest floor aren't the only flowers around. Many trees also flower in the spring. Most trees have small flowers we do not notice, but some trees grow beautiful flowers. Flowering dogwood trees have large white flowers. Redbud trees have many tiny pink flowers that cover their branches. Redbud and flowering dogwood trees are often planted in people's yards. Can you find one of these trees in your neighborhood?

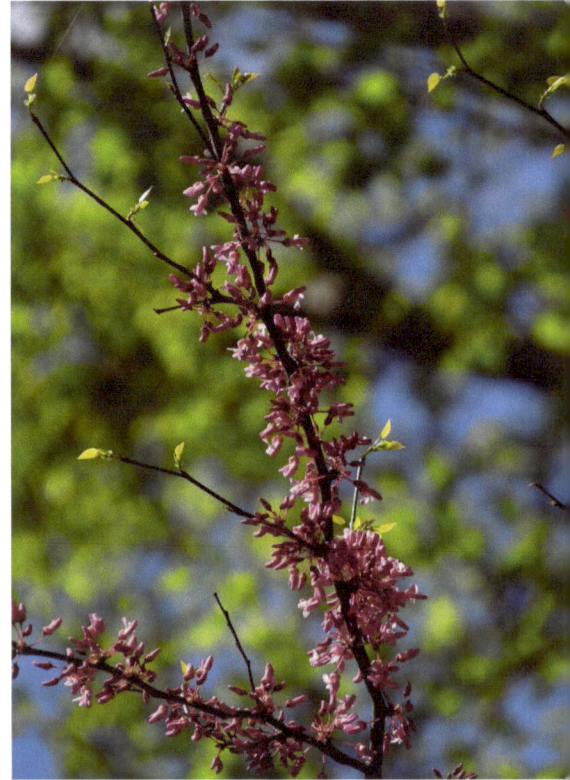

For Parents and Teachers

Here are some questions to ask your young explorers when you are out in the woods.

Q1: What color are these flowers?

Q2: Why do you think these flowers have such bright colors?

Q3: Does this plant have stems that are hairy or smooth?

Q4: Why do you think some plants have hairy stems?

Q5: How many petals does this flower have?

Q6: What does this flower smell like?

Q7: What insects do you see visiting these flowers?

Q8: Why do you think the insects are visiting the flowers? What are these insects doing when they visit the flowers?

Q9: Why do plants make nectar for insects?

Q10: Why do you think leaves are almost always green?

For Parents and Teachers

Here are a few answers for your young explorers.

A2: Flowers are brightly colored to attract pollinators. Insects like bumblebees and butterflies easily see the bright colors and know they can get food from the flowers.

A4: It is not unusual for plants to have hairy stems or leaves. Often plants are hairy to deter animals from eating them. Sometimes these hairs might produce a toxic substance that tastes bad. Other hairs are sharp, and may pierce a small insect. Hairs can also help plants be warmer or colder than the surrounding air.

A8: Pollinators usually visit flowers to collect nectar. Nectar is a sweet, sugary liquid that pollinators consume. Some pollinators also collect pollen. Pollen is a great source of protein for insects, especially for developing bees.

A9: Plants do not make nectar to be nice to insects. In order to make seeds, most flowers need pollen from another flower of the same species. Some plants rely on insects to carry this pollen. Insects visit flowers to drink nectar, and pollen will stick to the insects. The insects are likely to visit many flowers, and carry the pollen with them.

A10: Plants make food inside a small structure called a chloroplast. Chloroplasts are green, and they are why leaves are green.

Glossary

Dispersed – to be carried away and spread apart

Flower bud – part of a plant that will grow into a flower

Invasive plant – a non-native plant that grows quickly and replaces native species

Nectar – a sugary drink plants make to attract pollinators

Nectar guide – a pattern on flower petals that show animals where nectar and pollen can be found

Nectar robber – an animal that takes nectar by chewing a small hole through the flower. They do not carry pollen from one plant to the next

Petal - colorful flower parts that attract pollinators

Pistil - the center part of a flower that will make seeds if it receives pollen.

Pollen – a fine powder that flowers need to make seeds

Pollinate – when a flower receives pollen so it can make seeds

Pollinator – an animal that carries pollen from one flower to another

Sepal - part of a plant that protects flower buds and supports open flowers. They are often green and look like little leaves under a flower.

Stamen - part of the flower that releases pollen

Stem - part of a plant that supports the leaves and flowers

Your Plant List

Record each plant you discover.

- [ ] Liverleaf
- [ ] Bloodroot
- [ ] Skunk cabbage
- [ ] Rue anemone
- [ ] Dutchman's breeches
- [ ] Squirrel corn
- [ ] Trout lily
- [ ] Mayapple
- [ ] Spring beauty
- [ ] Trillium
- [ ] Cut-leaved toothwort
- [ ] Blue cohosh

- [ ] Wild geranium
- [ ] Virginia bluebells
- [ ] Wild blue phlox
- [ ] Jack-in-the-pulpit
- [ ] Wild ginger
- [ ] Violets
- [ ] Wild columbine
- [ ] Squawroot
- [ ] Garlic mustard
- [ ] Fiddleheads
- [ ] Redbud
- [ ] Dogwood

www.ingramcontent.com/pod-product-compliance
Lightning Source LLC
Chambersburg PA
CBHW041238040426
42445CB00004B/66